ARCHIBALD
MacLEISH
SCRATCH

SCRATCH

ARCHIBALD MacLEISH

SCRATCH

suggested by
Stephen Vincent Benét's
short story
"The Devil and Daniel Webster"

19 71

HOUGHTON MIFFLIN COMPANY BOSTON

To Stuart Ostrow and Peter Hunt

FOREWORD

Stephen Vincent Benét's "The Devil and Daniel Webster" is
one more proof that myths are made of time as well as tales. It
first appeared in *The Saturday Evening Post* in 1936, a short
story of unusual delight but a short story notwithstanding. Today
it is a fable from which men quarry plays.

Everyone knows the tale. Jabez Stone, a New Hampshire
farmer, fed up with the hardscrabble life of the rocky hills, sells
his soul to the Devil for a mess of prosperity and then, when
the bill of sale falls due, applies to Daniel Webster, the great
forensic orator of the time, to save his hide. Webster agrees: "If
two New Hampshire men aren't a match for the Devil . . ."
So the case is tried at midnight at the old Stone farm. The Devil
provides a jury of the dead and damned and a judge to match,
but Webster's eloquence convinces even them and the verdict
is returned for Jabez Stone — with the result that the Devil
hasn't been seen in New Hampshire since. "I'm not talking
about Massachusetts or Vermont."

All this sounded to the nineteen-thirties, and was intended to
sound, like Yankee folklore. The humor was Yankee humor
which is still the tartest in the world: sharp and cool and wry as
a Baldwin apple. The characters were Yankee characters: Benét's
Devil would have been an ornament to any cracker barrel in
Chocorua. The lawsuit was a tall tale in the grand style of the
old Northeast, which got its salt from the sea, its rum from Bar-
bados and its imagination from the dying embers of the long,
wild, winter nights. The story became a Yankee classic.

But it was not yet a myth. That mysterious metamorphosis

came with changes in the times and first, perhaps, with what economists call the Age of Affluence. The Republic was suddenly full of men and women who had sold their souls, and not for necessities of life but for its comforts, its amenities — for a mess of prosperity-on-credit. Jabez Stone was no longer a New Hampshire farmer. He rode in every other Cadillac in town.

That was one metamorphosis. The second involved the supernatural: the Devil changed. Benét's folksy Old Scratch had been a conventional devil concerned merely with the recruitment of souls for a hell in which no one any longer believed. The new Devil of the sixties had discovered — not without help from fashionable writers — that belief in hell was reviving everywhere and that, if only love of life could be turned into contempt for living, hope into despair, the entire planet would dissolve into that cistern of self-pity where Godot never comes. Hell would then take over the whole world.

The third change, and the most radical so far as Benét's story went, was in Webster himself. In the tale as told in the thirties Webster had appeared merely as a trial lawyer. There was no occasion in those years to recall his historic career as senator. The great issue which had dominated that career and given it its tragic dimensions had been dead for seventy years — or so the men of the thirties would have told you. The Union for which Webster struggled had been "saved" by the Civil War. The slavery he abhorred had "ended." Above all, the contradiction at the heart of the American Proposition had been "resolved." No one in 1936 suggested that the country had still to choose between Liberty and Union — between individual freedom and stable government.

By 1970, however, though the Union still survived and slavery had — ostensibly — disappeared, it was no longer certain that the contradiction at the heart was healed. There were indications that it might have become more cancerous than in Webster's day. Men on the contemporary left echoed the New England Abolitionists who put Liberty first and Union after, and were as ready as the Abolitionists had ever been to bring the Republic down in the name of freedom. At the same time there were those on the contemporary right who repeated the Copperhead cries of Union first and Liberty nowhere, proposing to surrender human freedom itself to something they called law-and-order.

And the voices on both sides were strident and implacable — as angry as voices had ever been before the Civil War. To the left, the Union had become "the System" and thus contemptible. To the right, Liberty was "permissiveness" — something to be derided and suppressed.

With this shift in the winds it was no longer possible, even in the world of Benét's fable, for Webster to play the simple role of lawyer. The historic Webster demanded to be heard, for the historic Webster was the one man in that tragic time who had dared to face the contradiction. He understood, as even Emerson did not, that there is no choice between Liberty and Union in America — that what the American people had done when they established their self-governing state was to refuse to choose between the freedom of man and the government of men — what they had done indeed was precisely the opposite: *to choose both.* Webster had said so: "Liberty *and* Union, now and forever, one and inseparable."

It is because these words speak to our own condition so explicitly, rebuke our official cynicism and shallowness so stingingly, that Benét's Webster turns into history's Webster as we read the story now. And it is for this same reason that when Webster runs his historic risk and accepts the scorn which history for generations has heaped upon him, the story turns to myth, for the destiny of a people is then caught up in it.

Archibald MacLeish
Conway, Massachusetts

SCRATCH

PROLOGUE

We are in an old New England barn: huge beams, high roof, cracked boards. A single shaft of early morning sunlight rakes down from panes of glass above the huge door, motes of hay dust floating in it. There is discarded furniture about and broken farm machinery and, on the walls and in the corners, relics and mementoes of the first century of the Republic: a torn flag with thirteen stars, a bust of General Washington, a chaise with three wheels, the figurehead of a ship. To our right, motionless in a chair, is what might be a seated statue of Daniel Webster — a magnificent old white-haired man in the famous blue coat and canary waistcoat. To our left, seated opposite Webster, is a second white-haired immobile figure in a flowery waistcoat of the era before the Civil War. He has an incongruous pouch over his shoulder and his face is fixed in a saturnine grin. Between the two stands a youngish man in the business uniform of the eighteen-fifties. We have the impression he had been speaking before the curtain rose — that he is going on from something said before.

Jabez: *looking up at the shaft of sunlight*

. . . it's morning . . .

. . . I'm still here . . .

he turns to the figure on our right

Mr. Webster!

louder

> *Mr. Webster!*

Webster: *rousing*

> Good morning, Jabez.

Jabez: It *is* — it's morning!

Scratch: *rousing in his turn*

> *Morning!* Whoever heard of *welcoming* the morning?

> *stretch*

> Beastliest moment of the blasted day! The blind-ing light!

> *groan*

> Night's the time to wait for in this filthy world — the evening's dim refusal — the denying dark.

Jabez: *to the audience*

> Mr. Webster loves the mornings. The Devil . . .

> *a gesture toward the figure on our left*

> . . . don't. And there are other things they can't agree on.

he comes down stage

> The greatest law case ever argued in the country
> — it never got written down in the books, but
> the greatest law case — was tried between them
> once . . .

gesture toward the barn behind him

> . . . here in this very barn.

Webster: Nip and tuck . . .

Scratch: And no holds barred!

*They bow to each other. A sharp, brisk, brassy bell — a ringside
signal, we think, until it goes clanging on and on and we know
what it is: an old-fashioned call to breakfast. We are in:*

SCENE ONE

The kitchen at Marshfield at dawn on a July day in 1850. Lantern light. Huge table. Red-and-white checked cloth. Coffeepot as big as a milk pail, cream in great pint pitchers, mountains of butter, bowls of summer flowers. The hired girl, buxom and crisp as a trayful of laundry, circles the table with last-minute spoons, plates, napkins, cups. Mrs. Weston, arms under her apron, surveys the scene from the door to the summer kitchen.

Scraping and stamping of barnyard boots. Weston comes in with Wright and the rest of the hired men.

Voices: Morning, ma'am.

              Bid ye good morning, Mrs. Weston.

              Fresh bread this morning: I can smell it.

              Good morning, ma'am. I'll have my usual beef-
              steak. Fried.

Mrs. Weston: You will if I happen to think of it, Porter.

Voices: Popovers! As I live and breathe, *popovers!*

              I'll stick to poi. There's blueberry poi this morn-
              ing. Susan told me — didn't you, Susan?

Susan: I *never*, Mrs. Weston!

Mrs. Weston: What would it matter, child? — there *is*.

4

A great scraping of chair legs on the floor; clatter of plates, knives, spoons; cream pitchers go sailing back and forth from hand to hand; the hired girl swings around the table with platters of steak, eggs, bacon, pie — and all the while the big pine chair at the head of the table stands magnificently empty. A tuneless voice off. Webster appears.

Webster: Ah, the mornings! The mornings!

> *He takes his seat in the noble old Windsor chair, shakes out his napkin with a flourish; disappears behind the hired girl pouring his coffee, serving his butter, passing him popovers; emerges again.*

Weston: Never miss a morning do you, Mr. Webster?

Webster: *his mouth full of popover*

> Good morning, Mrs. Weston! Good morning! Magnificent popovers! You remember how I love them.

Mrs. Weston's voice: *off*

> I remember how you eat them anyway.

> *She appears.*

> Good morning. We're happy to have you home.

Webster: And I'm happy to be here. You've no idea how happy.

to Weston

No, I never miss a sunrise here at Marshfield. Coffee, Porter, please.

Peterson enters, crosses, head down, to the foot of the table.

Good morning, Seth: haven't seen you since December, have I? Day we walked down to the river at dawn with the tide in and the marshes covered and not a breath of wind on the water anywhere — ice-blue and the port deserted, the lobster houses boarded up — only the Canada geese on the still river and, out against the sun, wild swans. Remember that?

No answer. Peterson sits down.

Webster, momentarily puzzled, turns back to Weston.

No, never miss them here and not often in Washington. I know the morning. I am acquainted with it and I love it, fresh and sweet as it is, a daily new creation breaking forth . . .

The girl swings around again.

Pie? I don't care if I do. Just a bit of it — a quarter maybe. They look like low-bush blueberries. Nature's greatest gift to New England. Next to the bluefish, Seth, of course.

Wright: *sourly: a sidewise look down the table at Peterson.*

6

Next to the Yankees!

Webster: *to Wright*

Well, the country Yankees maybe: not the Bos-
tonians. *They* never see the sunrise in their lives.

Weston: Except in winter when it rises 'long toward noon.

Wright: Nor the nights either with those streetlights they
keep blazing, dusk to dawn.

Webster: Oh, the nights! Who cares about the nights?
Night is a wilderness you're meant to sleep
through, the way you sleep through pine scrub on
the cars . . .

a chuckle

So long, that is, as you don't dream. I dreamt last
night. First time in a dog's age. I dreamt . . .

the laughter fades from his voice

. . . something or someone leaned so close above
me I could hear its . . . heart.
Enormous heart beats . . . I was terrified . . . I
couldn't *move* — breathe even.

Pause, silence

I seemed to know, the way you do in dreams, that
what was standing — leaning over me — was
. . . evil.

7

Not just bad or frightening but evil. *Evil!* The way the stench of death is death.

I knew what it was, of course . . . when I woke up.

Peterson: *under his breath*

The Devil stalking you.

Wright: *to Peterson*

For God's sake don't start *that* again.

Peterson: They say his heart beats something awful when he gets you down.

Weston: *to Webster*

Of course you knew what it was. The sea. The rut of the sea on the north beach.

Webster: Rut of the sea. I've heard it often enough when the wind drops after a blow like yesterday's. *There's* a word for Mr. Peterson to remember. Rut. Latin *rota* meaning repetition: successive surges shattering on the sand. Too slow for a heart, of course, but in a dream . . .

Peterson: Not too slow for *his* heart. They say it beats the way a turtle's . . .

Mrs. Weston appears beyond the table.

Webster: *to Peterson*

What's this you're saying — or not saying?

Peterson: *back to his steak*

Nothing . . .

looking up at Webster: a slow look

I've been reading, that's all. In the papers.

Mrs. Weston: *taking charge, throwing the helm sharp over*

I suppose you'll be leaving us quick as you came, Mr. Webster, now you're in the Cabinet again.

Webster: Drat the Cabinet! The only Cabinet I want a part of is your husband and Porter Wright and this seagoing Satanist, Seth, discussing your buckwheat cakes in your well-scrubbed kitchen with sausages maybe, if Mr. Weston ever kills that pig and smokes it as I told him.

This is the expansive moment after breakfast: He leans back, talking for the pleasure of it, the men at ease in their chairs, the girl and Mrs. Weston beyond.

We've done more State Department business here in Marshfield than anyone in Washington ever guessed. Maybe some of you recall my negotiations with the British when I was Secretary of State before. I settled every question of magni-

9

tude in the Washington discussions except one, the most important question of all — the fisheries. That topic I reserved to take up with Mr. Peterson here, on Ned's Ground, off Bluefish Rock, at six on a September morning — a warm, still, smoky day with the wind southeast and a swell running.

Peterson: Mostly halibut as I recall — one or two quite sizable.

Webster: *a slow rich laugh*

It was there, on that occasion, that Mr. Peterson delivered himself of the great political principle which has guided my efforts ever since. "There is sometimes," said Seth, "an odd fish too smart to take the bait. You must try him with the *naked hook*. The smarter he is the quicker he'll swallow it."

Peterson: Have it your own way, Mr. Webster. It wasn't political principles we were talking about; it was President Tyler's troubles. I said the fault was in the Congress. They ought to take right hold, man-fashion, and do up the public business. Mr. Tyler was not to blame for being President: if President Harrison hadn't died he never would have been, and nobody better pleased than himself. He understood what it was to be *Vice*-President and he liked it. A *Vice*-President, he knew, is like a cod: a bottom feeder — never ought to be seen at the surface. Mr. Tyler liked that kind of job.

Webster: As every senator likes it: bottom feeders to the last man!

Peterson: Ha! Senators! More like marlin. Dancing around on their tails to show they're there.

Webster: But you *like* marlin, Seth. You know you like them. You'll let a blue go any day to watch the marlin leap and glance and glitter and go down, smothered in sea surge.

Peterson: Oh yes, to watch them break. But not with the hook in the mouth, Mr. Webster. Not when they try to throw the hook. That, I don't care to look at.

Mrs. Weston appears again, her hands under her apron.

That's for those tiptoe fish, all flash and splash and not worth having when you take them.

The really big ones stay below. And pull. Like horses. Nothing can get them up until their hearts break. They don't . . . quit!

Wright: Stop him, Weston!

Webster: Careful what you say of senators, Peterson. I was a senator myself last week.

Mrs. Weston: And for some weeks before that.

Weston: Not to say years.

Mrs. Weston:	Long as anyone in *this* house can remember.
Peterson:	Good one, too.
Wright:	*Good!* There was never better. Calhoun and Clay were minnows to him! Fry fish!
Webster:	Don't bully him, Porter. Good, in Seth's vocabulary, means what it says. I'm grateful for it.
Wright:	I suppose you're grateful for the rest of it, too!
Webster:	The rest of it?
Wright:	The Devil getting you down: getting the best of you.
Weston:	That's enough, Wright.
Peterson:	You ought to read the papers, Porter. It wasn't me who tossed the Devil into Mr. Webster's dream. Every respected writer in the Commonwealth has had his say about it since that speech of Mr. Webster's four months ago. Seventh March, eighteen-fifty! They know that date, every one of them.
Wright:	Can't you stop him, Weston? All day long . . .
Peterson:	Even Mister Greenleaf Whittier, that old, bald, blatting, bleating sheep!
Webster:	Seth! Seth! Don't let them make you angry.

Peterson: They ought to make *you* angry, Daniel. You
              know what Mr. Whittier says? "When faith is
              lost, when honor dies, the man is dead." That's
              you, he means. He calls his poem "Ichabod" —
              any Yankee knows what "Ichabod" intends to
              say. It's in First Samuel: "The Glory is de-
              parted."

          pause

              Your glory, Daniel . . . Ours . . .

Webster: All right, Seth, but don't get angry — not with
              them — me if you have to, but not them. Times
              like these turn even the most reasonable men to
              bigots. They mount upon their sense of duty as
              upon a war horse and go galloping off over every
              other man and every other duty that stands in
              their way. What would be differences of opinion
              at any other time become differences between
              good and evil, between Heaven and Hell.

Peterson: But there *are* differences between Heaven and
              Hell, Daniel, and there *is* right and there *is* wrong
              and every now and then a duty *does* turn up that
              you have to mount and ride like a war horse.

          Pause: Peterson gets control of himself

              Why did you have to say it, Daniel? In the Sen-
              ate . . .

Webster: I said a number of things in the Senate. I said

13

there were grievances on both sides, North and South, and men exploiting those grievances on both sides, exaggerating them.

Peterson: About the law.

Webster: I said the law must be enforced.

Peterson: You said the *Fugitive Slave Law* must be enforced.

Wright: *No!* I won't sit here and . . .

Chairs are pushed back, voices break in — and Mrs. Weston, all sails set, comes wheeling around the table.

Webster: You *will* sit here!

Mrs. Weston: Excuse me, Mr. Webster, but he won't. Nor the rest of you neither. This is not the Senate. This is an honest woman's kitchen with dishes to wash for seven men and a floor to mop after muddy boots and a lamb stew to start for a twelve o'clock dinner and . . .

Weston: Not to speak of a day's work to be planned . . .

Webster: *both hands up in surrender*

Very well. Very well. Give us a moment, Mrs. Weston, and Seth and I will have it out. With blunt words. At four feet. But first, the day . . .

Webster and Weston hit the words together.

> Proverbs twenty-eight, verse twenty-three. "Be diligent to know the state of thy flocks and look well to thy herds."

The laughter of relief

Webster: Specifically, take the oxen to the beach for kelp. Never forget, it was fish, kelp and barn manure made Marshfield what it is: work it in! Work it in! Don't mind the ladies. Tell 'em it's Marshfield roses they smell.

Weston: We'll tell the ladies you say so, Mr. Secretary.

Webster: What else?

Wright: Your horses, Mr. Webster.

Webster: Ah, yes, my roans. Liberty and Union. Best we've ever seen at Marshfield or anywhere else in the Commonwealth.

> *pause*

> Well, we all get older . . . get old. At least they went together. Sad though . . .

Silence

Wright: They ought to be buried before — well, the sun gets *too* high.

Webster:	But bury them with all the honors of war. Bury them standing side by side in the same grave with their shoes on and their halters buckled. Choose a site by the sea where you can hear the sound. A slate stone. Black not gray. With an inscription . . .
Weston:	We thought we'd use those words of yours every schoolboy knows: "Liberty and Union, now and forever, one and inseparable."
Peterson:	You won't get 'em side by side in the same grave if you do. Not now. Not anymore. Not since that speech of the seventh March. Union comes first and Liberty afterward these days. *Way* afterward! So far after you'll have to bury them nose to tail. Liberty's nose to Union's tail . . .
Wright:	Can't you let up on it even for one . . .
Webster:	All right, Seth: we'll talk about it — try to. As for the rest of you, dig the grave, get the kelp in, dress the pasture . . .

Weston turns to go, the others following.

> . . . Oh, and about that epitaph. We'll change it. Not so much in respect for Mr. Peterson's emotions as in respect for the roans. They deserve the durability of Latin. Chalk *this* on your slate and cut it later:

Siste Viator!
Viator te major hic sistet.

Which I take to mean — Seth will correct me:
he's been talking Latin all *through* breakfast —

Wait traveler!
A greater traveler than you waits here.

Appropriate, don't you think, Mr. Peterson?
We're all travelers in this place — though we
don't know yet from where to where.

Siste Viator!

Weston and his men crowd out the door.

over his shoulder to the summer kitchen

Magnificent breakfast, Mrs. Weston. As always.
Except for the maple syrup and that was the best
in seven years.

Rattle of dishes off for answer

*Webster turns to Seth, who sits in a dogged Yankee
silence, head down.*

It's true too. This was a great year for maple, Mr.
Weston tells me. Fine, cold nights in February:
sun thaws at noon. Sugar weather.

No response from Peterson

17

It's the weather not the calendar that counts.
Remember that sensible Latin advice to farmers?
— plow naked and sow naked? You know what
that means.

Peterson: *head still down*

Means you shouldn't crowd the season. No use
calling it spring till it warms up.

Webster: That's good advice still, Mr. Peterson. Wait till
you know where you are before you lay about you.
And don't just take the season from the books.
Our ancestors used to plant corn by the almanac:
May first, Old Style; May eleventh, New. The
Indians knew better. They put their corn in the
ground when the new leaf on the white oak was
as big as a mouse's ear. Years vary.

Peterson: Don't tell that to *me*, Mr. Webster. Tell it to the
men who *write* the books. Mr. Greenleaf Whit-
tier. Dr. Oliver Wendell Holmes. Mr. Emerson.
Mr. Thoreau. I just *read*. I'm the hired man.
Authority on . . . barn manure . . . horseshit . . .

Webster: Trout. Woodcock. Black duck. Not to mention halibut, cod, blues.

Peterson: *And* horseshit. Don't leave out the horseshit.
That's what you think, so say it!

Webster: I think when you talk about that speech of mine

and ask me why I urged the enforcement of the
law . . .

Peterson: *jerking his head up at last*

Of the *Fugitive Slave Law!*

Webster: . . . you don't know what you're talking about.
The Constitution of the United States enjoins the
enforcement of such laws. Persons held to service
in one state and escaping into another must be
returned to servitude.

Peterson: Which is why the abolitionists down in Boston
call the Constitution an agreement with Hell and
a covenant with death.

Webster: Abolitionists! Your abolitionist is the worst of
those fanatic riders of the blind horse of ungov-
ernable duty. He knows his right is right and
everyone else's right is wrong and he proposes
that his right shall triumph even if he brings the
country down — even if thousands upon thousands of young men, North as well as South and
South as well as North, must perish beneath those
iron hooves.

pause

Think of the Union, Seth. Think what will happen to the Union if this agony goes on.

19

Peterson: *his voice low, almost gentle*

> And you, Daniel. Think of the slaves! Think
> what *has* happened to the slaves!

pause

> And to their masters! . . .

pause

> And to us who share this continent with their
> masters! . . .

Webster: Precisely! To us who share this continent with
their masters! Oh, I wish I could make you see it,
Seth.

The Constitution, like everything else in life, like
life itself, is a compromise. I've told you again
and again: all legislation, all government, all
society, is formed upon the principle of mutual
concessions, politeness, comity, courtesy.

Peterson: So are all lies, all cheats, all . . .

fumbling for the words

> . . . degrading arrangements. Don't you see,
> Daniel, why they bring the Devil into it? — why
> they say you've yielded to the Tempter? They
> mean just that. They mean *you've* compromised
> — and compromise in these parts is where the
> Devil gets his thumb in and the girl rolls over.

Webster:	Compromised! Of course we've compromised. We compromised in Missouri. We compromised in South Carolina. We've been compromising for a generation because, for a generation, secession has been a possibility, and secession means civil war.
Peterson:	But they mean *you*. *You*, Daniel! They mean *you've* compromised. Here's Dr. Holmes. He calls it . . .

fishing in his overall pocket, pulling out a clipping

	. . . "The Statesman's Secret." He even knows the bait the Tempter's offered you . . .
Webster:	Bait!
Peterson:	The Presidency.
Webster:	Fairly open secret! There isn't a four-year-old in Massachusetts doesn't know I want the Presidency. It is the greatest office in the world and I am but a man, sir. I want it. I want it! And I hope to have it even now.

Is that the end of it? |
Peterson:	Of Dr. Holmes, yes.
Webster:	Who else bears witness?
Peterson:	Mr. Emerson.

Webster's face tightens: pause

Webster: Well, are you going to let me hear it?

Peterson: *gently*

If you wish to hear it.
  "Why did all manly gifts in Webster fail?
  He wrote on Nature's grandest brow, For Sale!"

Silence. Webster staring into Peterson's face, not seeing it

That's what they're saying, Daniel . . . Forgive
me for . . . knowing it.

Webster: For sale! My opinions, my beliefs, for *sale!* What
right has Mr. Emerson to say so? What act of
mine would justify such — calumny?

Peterson: Are you asking *me?*

Webster: In Mr. Emerson's absence.

Peterson: He means that speech.

Webster: That I offered, in that speech, to sell my principles for the Presidency?

Peterson: More or less.

Webster: Is that what *you* think, Seth? Is that what you've
been saying? — or not saying?

Peterson: I've fished with you too often, Daniel. I know how you stay with . . . your convictions.

Webster: That's not good enough.

Peterson: No, it's not good enough. You've never let up on a fish to my knowledge but in that speech . . .

Webster: I let up on slavery?

Peterson: Put it that you . . . changed your mind.

Webster: And you want to know why? — you and Mr. Emerson.

Peterson: Mr. Emerson seems to know already.

Webster: Yes: not even God can tell Mr. Emerson. But maybe Daniel Webster can tell you.

pause

I tried to say it in the Senate when I rose that day to speak.

"Mr. President," I said, "I wish to speak to you today not as a Massachusetts man, nor as a Northern man, but as an American, a member of the Senate of the United States. I speak today for the preservation of the Union.

pause

"Hear me for my cause.

pause

"Hear . . ."

Peterson: *brusquely*

I know the speech!

Silence

Webster:　　Look, Seth. I want you to see something. A bright day — bright morning. March is often fine in Washington. Not like the blasted season here — the late sleet. We are in the Senate chamber — sunlight — the room full — not only the senators' desks and the galleries and the doors and aisles but the whole room: visitors everywhere — women mostly — hats like flowers in the sun — lovely dresses. They are perched on senators' chairs, on the steps to the Vice-President's seat — everywhere. The great room is fragrant with them . . .

pause

Walker of Wisconsin has the floor — he was speaking when we adjourned yesterday — but he yields to me.

pause

24

I had waited seven days to speak. I suppose I was nearly broken down with anxiety and waiting and the words of the old President, John Quincy Adams, were ringing in my ears. He'd told me in forty-eight, before he died, that he'd give the Union five years more and the years were running out. I stood there looking at the sunlight on the dresses and counting the years. California was about to enter the Union as free soil and New Mexico was certain to enter the Union as free soil and Oregon would follow them in, and if California and New Mexico and the rest entered the Union as free soil, the slave states would go out. They had already called a convention to meet in Nashville, in June.

He strikes his fist into his hand.

In *Nashville! Over the bones of Andrew Jackson!*

IIe lifts his head.

If the slave states went out it meant war.

pause

I stood there counting the years on my fingers.

Silence

You asked me why I had to say what I said. I saw in the flooding sunlight in that crowded room, among the pretty hats and lifted faces, the Union shattered . . . and the stain of blood.

Silence

You tell me I have changed my mind. You seem to say I have changed my mind about slavery. I have not changed my mind about slavery. I detest slavery. I regard slavery as a great moral and political evil, a degraded and degrading evil, degrading to master as to slave, more degrading to master than to slave . . .

I abhor slavery!

Peterson: *speaking with difficulty*

I know. You couldn't change your mind about slavery any more than a cow could change her mind about thistles. But you *have* changed, Daniel. You've changed about . . . the Union.

Webster: *The Union!* I love the Union. The whole of my public life has been devoted to the preservation of the Union. Years I should have spent at the Supreme Court bar arguing famous cases for fat fees to keep my wife in silks and Marshfield solvent I spent on the Senate floor instead, in Senate committees, cloakrooms, boardinghouses, wearing the carpets threadbare for my single cause. I could have been a rich man, Seth: not, as I am, half bankrupt and dependent on the contributions of my constituents. But, oh my friend . . .

his hand on Seth's sleeve

I love the Union.

Peterson: I know you do. Maybe that's what I'm saying, Daniel. People can change about a thing by loving it as easy as by hating it. A woman who loves her house can come to love it, not for her husband's comfort or her children's joy, but for itself — order and neatness for the sake of order and neatness. You know what that does to a family. The same thing can happen with a country — with a man and his country — with you and the Union. You love the Union: you always have. But once you loved it for the kind of life a man could live in it. Now you love it for itself. Because it's powerful. Because it's rich.

The cud is too bitter for Peterson to swallow.

Maybe you'll even come to love it for its slavery — because it's rich in slaves.

Webster wheels on him, black with rage.

No, hear me, Daniel! Hear me . . . for my cause. It's not your hatred of slavery which has changed. It's the way you love the Union — what you think of when you say you love the Union. Once you thought of men — *free men* . . .

Webster: Will you let me say for myself what I think of when I name the Union? I think of the failure

27

and chaos and misery under the old Confederation of States into which I was born. I think of the prosperity and power of the new Union of the States, its flag on every sea, its frontiers on the coasts of a vast continent. I think of the mortal danger that all our hopes, all our prospects of greatness, may collapse in war. It is of this I think — all this — when I name the Union. And when I think of this, all this, I swear to Almighty God that the Union shall not fail: that the preservation of the Union shall come first . . .

Peterson: First . . . ?

Webster: Before *everything!*

Peterson: Before human liberty?

Webster: Human liberty! Human liberty! People talked about human liberty in the old Confederation. They ranted against the Constitution in the name of human liberty. And how much human liberty did they have? Just about enough to want for everything — to hunger — to quarrel, state against state — to be miserable.

              What's human liberty without a country?

Peterson: Or a country . . . without human liberty?

Webster: All this . . . all this is ghostly abstraction! Ghostly abstraction! The Union is real. It exists . . . trades . . . traffics . . . builds . . . expands . . .

Peterson: And Liberty isn't real? Is that what you're saying?

Webster: Not until you make it real. Not until you give
              it a country . . . a people. There has to be a
              country first before there's freedom in a country.
              And a country's difficult, Seth: it takes work
              to make it — time — patience — intelligence —
              good will. Generations have to give their lives to
              it. You know that. Think of the great men,
              living and dead, who gave their lives, their blood,
              their hope, to make this country. Think of *that*
              before you tear it down to right a wrong . . .
              however grievous.

Seth sits silent staring at his hands.

              Think of the Union, Seth — how she stands
              there!

Silence

Peterson: I'm thinking of her, Daniel. But all I seem to see
              is . . . men. Black men. White men. Oh, men
              aren't much, I grant you. Men will lie, kill, forni-
              cate like rabbits, follow each other's follies like
              so many sheep. Still, they're men. They matter.

Webster: They matter with a government to govern them.
              Freedom under government. Without it they're
              . . . a mob!

              I've seen mobs, Mr. Peterson.

Peterson: And I've seen men and maybe that's the differ-
ence!

*Peterson starts out, turns, pauses behind Webster. A
gesture of affection*

I love the Union dear as you do, Daniel . . .

Webster stirs.

. . . well, *almost* . . . but not for itself. I love
it for its men.

Silence. Webster staring at the wall

I suppose a statesman *has* to count by govern-
ments but a Yankee don't: he counts by heads,
by people.

straightening up to go

You're a Yankee, Daniel. Count by men and
. . . shame the Devil.

He goes out.

The light fades. We are in:

SCENE TWO

Webster's backyard at Marshfield. High noon. Webster drowsing in his chair under the gigantic elms. Flickering light and shade. Scratch appears out of shadow into sun.

Scratch: Mr. Webster . . . ?

Webster lifts his heavy head, peers around him in the dazzle, misses Scratch, then sees him.

Webster: I am Daniel Webster. You, sir?

Scratch: You don't *know* me?

Webster: Should I?

Scratch: Most men do . . . in *your* profession.

Webster: Hardly a compliment to you. The kind of men most lawyers know . . .

Scratch: Did I mention lawyers, Mr. Webster? I apologize.

Webster: Ah, of course — a politician. I should have known it by your . . . consummate effrontery. I

31

was asleep, sir! . . . *attempting*, that is, to fall asleep.

Scratch: Attempting! Under the elm trees at the flood of noon and snoring like a double-ended saw!

Webster: Your business, sir? You tell me you're a politician . . .

Scratch: *I* did not say so. You did. But the term will serve. I find myself at home with politicians. They speak my language. Constituents! — they love to talk of their constituents. So do I.

Webster: And yours, of course, are numerous.

Scratch: Quite numerous. A clear majority.

Webster: I'm sure. No politician worthy of the name claims less.

Scratch: And Daniel Webster is a politician worthy of the name. What majority does *he* claim?

Webster: *closing his eyes*

None. I am a candidate for nothing . . . but the arms of Morpheus.

Scratch: Candidate for nothing!

Webster: Nothing.

Scratch: Not even for the Pres-i-den-cy?

Webster: For no office!

Scratch: *pause: peering at Webster closely*

You *are* Daniel Webster?

Webster opens one eye.

But no, I have no need to ask. The whole world
knows that head, that bearing. "Nature's . . .

the exaggerated emphasis of quotation marks

. . . grandest brow!"

Webster: *sitting up*

I suggest, sir, it is time and more than time I
knew your name.

Scratch: To think that I should meet you face to face!
Secretary of State of the United States of Amer-
ica! Secretary for the second time!

Webster: Your name! In three words, sir: who are you?

Scratch: Oh, nothing as grand as Mr. Daniel Webster.
There are some, like you, no office elevates because they are above all office: some, like me, no
office seeks. Still, you have heard of me, I think
— spoken of me even.

33

Webster: Spoken of you! Then there must have been a
            name to speak by.

Scratch: Scratch was your preference, I believe. Just
            Scratch. No honorific — nothing — just plain
            Scratch. Not much to boast of as a name but
            still I have my little satisfactions — successes
            even. Though none, I hasten to confess, was ever
            as spectacular as this — as fabulous — unhoped
            for . . .

Webster: *This?*

Scratch: *This!*

        pause

            I think you understand me.

Webster stares at him in blank silence.

            Have I been too credulous?

Webster stares.

            There are always those who understand my busi-
            ness better than I do myself and rush to publicize
            my triumphs — I have long known that. But
            these were reputable witnesses: writers and the
            like of that — preachers — Boston preachers —
            even a Concord philosopher. We take that sort
            of testimony seriously where I come from. Re-
            spectfully, you might say. And never has a more

34

remarkable consensus been recorded. So I am told, and I believe it. They *all* agree.

Webster: They all agree on what, sir?

Scratch: *He begins a sort of morris dance among the elms, Webster following.*

Why, that you have . . . seen the light. Come 'round. Of course they use their own locutions: "yielded to the Tempter" is the ordinary phrase. But what they mean is clearly that you've seen the light — reached the only possible conclusion open to a realistic mind, an honest intelligence. It makes me — you could never guess *how* happy.

Webster: Now just one moment . . .

Scratch: No, no: they're right. I quite agree with them. You see I've read your famous speech. Magnificent achievement! That eloquent repudiation of your country's adolescent thetoric — the meretricious claptrap of its infant years — that nonsense about "Liberty." *Mankind* endowed by its Creator with certain "unalienable rights"!

Webster: *Just . . . one . . . moment . . .*

Scratch: "Unalienable rights"! What rights, I ask you, has mankind? Mr. Jefferson seemed to think it *wallowed* in them — at least he said so in his fatuous Declaration.

35

Webster: *One moment!*

Scratch: The dignity of man! The dignity of *man!* Think
of those mortal, momentary creatures, half the
weight and size of a sound calf, strutting around
in horse dung in the streets of Philadelphia talking of the dignity of Man!

The *dignity!* I ask you! *Think* of it . . .

Of *Man!*

He chokes with laughter, collapses into Webster's chair.

Webster: Thank you.

Scratch waves a helpless, apologetic hand at him.

And now, before this interesting conversation
loses itself in history altogether, or what you
seem to think is history, may I inquire once more
who you are? You say your name is Scratch.

Scratch: *pulling himself together*

No, no. They *call* me Scratch . . .

a grin

As they called you when you were young, Black
Dan . . . your complexion, of course. Your father's mother's family as I recall it. The Bachel-
ders. One of those fine old swarthy British strains
that go way back before the Britons. Back of the

36

golden Gaels. The Picts. Back to the first beginnings — lost beginnings in the prehistoric dark where all the greatness comes from. The originals! I have family connections of my own in those beginnings.

Webster: Have you indeed!

Scratch: I have. *In deed.* I do not lie about my genealogy. Or anything else for the matter of that. I tell the truth. Those who are not accusutomed to the truth — and they are numerous — take it for falsehood sometimes. But you, of course, are familiar with *that* phenomenon.

Webster: Forgive me if I seem persistent. You say they call you Scratch. You intimate we know each other.

Scratch: Oh, yes. We know each other, Mr. Webster.

Webster: *Scratch?* I have never so much as heard the name in thcsc parts nor up in New Hampshire either nor anywhere else in New England. And I know New England. I know New England better than most, I may say. Never, anywhere, in all New England, in sixty-eight years of unimpaired hearing and a better than average interest in what's being said to me — never have I heard of Scratch. Oh, "the Old Scratch" certainly, but then . . .

Scratch: Then?

Webster: It's not exactly what you'd call a patronymic. I mean, there are no families founded in those syllables. One talks of "the Old Scratch" in order not to speak of the unspeakable . . .

Scratch: You mean . . . ?

Webster: The Devil . . . naturally.

Scratch: *You* make no difficulty with the term, sir.

Webster: Ah, you find the word offensive? I withdraw it.

Scratch: Not in the least — not in the least offensive, Mr. Webster. No one likes to be . . . unspeakable. Not even . . .

   a slight bow

      . . . I

Webster: *staring at him*

   You ask me to believe . . .

Scratch: I do not ask you to believe anything. Unlike some I can think of . . .

He lifts his eyes to the sky above the elm tops.

   . . . I never ask anyone to believe. I find I have no need to.

Webster: Then . . . you mean . . .

a cough of astonished laughter

. . . *that's* who you are?

Webster begins to laugh: a slow, rich chuckle which goes out of control.

I thought we'd lost you centuries ago back on the other side in the old country fiddling around at midnight by the beds of dying kings and sick whores, and such-like prospects.

paroxysm of laughter

Forgive me if I seem uncivil but *you* . . . here! . . .

wiping his eyes

The Devil in General Washington's Republic!

Scratch: Where evil is of course unknown.

Webster: Forgive me, sir: I see I go too far. Let me put it this way: you'll find few prospects on this continent.

Scratch: Few perhaps, but not the least or worst. One I can think of has declared himself already. Four months and nineteen days ago he told the Senate of your great Republic that if forced to choose between the bright new world of Mr. Jefferson and the realities of what you . . . here . . . call . . .

39

whipping out a great red handkerchief and blowing an ironic blast

> life, he'd vote for life. Ah, if he'd only known what life *is*, Mr. Webster. What death is, I might add. But we will talk of all that later. There will be time enough to talk — well, not precisely *time* but . . .

Webster: If your account of Eternity, sir, is no more precise than your account of the Senate of the United States, you will give me leave to conclude that you have been in neither. I did not choose between Mr. Jefferson's great dream of Liberty — his bright new world, as you so justly call it — and the realities of politics. I did not repudiate Liberty!

Scratch: Quite right. Quite right. It was the abolition of slavery you repudiated.

another blast on the great red handkerchief

> Slavery, you pointed out, is in the *Constitution*. Oh, not by name, not by name, but *there*. You were recalling your country, as you have so often, to the facts. You are a great champion of the facts, Mr. Webster — the greatest champion of the facts the young Republic has ever had. Most of your countrymen prefer those fine, inflated paper bags of rhetoric. "Pursuit of happiness"! Who ever heard of the pursuit of happiness? *You* know what greatness in a country really is. Power! Not the gas balloons of paper aspiration but the *fact*

40

of power. National power and the national prosperity which is the means to power. Guns and gold.

Webster: I cannot remember that I mentioned either guns *or* gold . . . except to warn against the guns.

Scratch: Nor New England textile mills — their need for slave-grown cotton. Nor the need of slave-grown cotton for New England mills. And yet the Senate understood you and the clamor stopped.

Webster: I spoke for the preservation of the Union.

Scratch: And you persuaded them: even though it meant the preservation of something else as well — something Mr. Jefferson's Sacred Declaration promised to eradicate. Oh, you were right. You were altogether right. You were — you are — an honest man. You understand reality.

Webster turns his back on him.

Am I offensive? When a man so loves the truth as you do, Mr. Webster, he should welcome it in others. Particularly when it sheds such honor on himself. I admire you, Mr. Webster. More than that — I value you. I am, as I am sure you know, a — shall I say, collector? — of humanity . . .

He draws from an inside pocket of his coat a fat, yellow leather wallet, strokes it as he talks.

41

. . . examples of humanity. A fascinating hobby.
You have no notion what varieties exist — what
unexpected specimens. You, sir, I should take to
be a most remarkable find. Most remarkable.
Not only in yourself, your scope, your scale,
your . . . yes, your grandeur — twice the dimensions ordinarily reported — not only in yourself
but in your representative capacity — the thing
you . . .

lifting the leather wallet to conceal a smile

. . . the thing you stand for. If one could number *you* in his collection he could very well assert
he *had* your country!

Webster: I represent the Commonwealth of Massachusetts
— nothing more and nothing less. But I am also,
as a man, American and I love my country. When
the issue is the preservation of my country I speak
out. That is the issue now: whether this nation
shall survive or perish.

Scratch: Ah, you *did* speak out: you *did* declare the issue.
That was your great achievement, Mr. Webster
— your magnificent achievement. You and you
only understand what your Republic is: not a phi-
losopher's model of the rights of man, whatever
they may be, but just a . . . country — a political contraption like another. And you *said* so.
And, saying so, you brushed those smoldering,
red, incendiary words aside like coals upon a car-
pet and so saved the house.

Ah, Mr. Webster, Mr. Webster, there is nothing such a man as you does not deserve. Nothing he should not expect. With confidence.

I propose to see your expectations realized.

Webster: *You* propose!

Scratch: Why not? I am indebted to you, Mr. Webster.

     pause

Or do you mean you doubt my influence in such matters?

Webster: In what matters?

Scratch: Oh, the Baltimore Convention of your party.

Webster: *snort of laughter*

If you are what you say you are you'll *run* the Baltimore Convention!

Scratch: Precisely. And the nomination will be yours.

Webster: You make a dubious assumption.

Scratch: What assumption?

Webster: That I want the nomination to that office . . .

Scratch: Mr. *Webster!*

43

Webster: . . . at *your hands.*

Scratch: You must not be contemptuous, Mr. President.
                I offer you my help, no more. I ask for nothing.

Webster: There is a proverb — I take it you don't care for
                proverbs — but you'll bear with just this one.

Scratch: It depends upon the proverb.

Webster: "When the Old Scratch asks for nothing . . ."

Scratch: . . . nothing not already given . . .

Webster: That's not the proverb. "When the Old Scratch
                asks for nothing, pat your pockets: you've been
                robbed."

Scratch: And that's the answer to the proverb: you gave it
                me yourself. You've . . . *joined* me, Mr. Web-
                ster. Four months and nineteen days ago. All
                New England is agreed on that — the most intel-
                ligent Bostonians and nothing in Heaven or Earth
                — or elsewhere — is more intelligent than a Bos-
                tonian.

Webster rounds on him: black angry brows, stares in silence.

                Perhaps you do not follow me.

Webster: I *trust* I do not follow you . . .

Scratch: Why then . . . you *do!*

44

Webster: *backing him toward the gate*

> Because, if I were certain that I truly understood
> you, I'd fling you headlong out that gate, wit over
> watch chain with your boots to follow. Call your-
> self what you please — Old Scratch — the Prince
> of Darkness . . .

Scratch: Please, no poetry! I can't abide it!

He pulls out his wallet.

Webster: And put that wallet in your pocket! There's some-
              thing crawling on it. What are they? — roaches?

Scratch: Some have thought so . . . some still do. The
              Greeks decided they were moths, or like moths —
              butterflies probably.

Pause. Scratch examining the wallet

> Psyche, you remember, was the Attic term.

Webster: Psyche! The soul? You don't pretend . . .

Scratch: Precisely. I do not pretend.

Webster: . . . those are human souls you have . . .

Scratch: "Collected" is the word I use myself.

Webster: . . . not here, though. Not in Massachusetts.

Scratch: Too small you think? No, no, quite up to stand-
                 ard. Not *your* standard, naturally. Not, at least,
                 when you attain the Presidency. How does Dr.
                 Holmes express it?

                 "Build thee more stately mansions, oh my soul."

                 Perhaps he hasn't said it yet but when *you* fill the
                 White House . . .

Webster: I make no question of their size but of their ori-
                 gin. Even the Devil out of Hell himself could
                 take no souls in these United States.

Scratch: Ah? Because your country's new, you trust the
                 goodness of the Universe? Well . . .

                 He snaps the wallet shut and crams it into his pocket.

                 . . . others have trusted it before you, Mr. Web-
                 ster.

Webster: Perhaps, but not *my* fellow countrymen. We *be-
                 lieve* in goodness but we *trust* ourselves. My fa-
                 ther, when he raised his roof far up the Merri-
                 mack and lit his fire, watched his smoke ascending,
                 as he told me, nearer the North Star than that of
                 any other of His Majesty's New England sub-
                 jects. He took his bearings by the stars but
                 squared his logs himself. We still do in America.
                 We swim white water like the trout in spring: a
                 plunging torrent where an unknown age rushes
                 upon its destiny. We have the West before us.
                 We tell our future, not by calendars of years but

by the great savannas still unplowed, the centuries of uncut forests.

As for the rest . . . we fear no evil but our own and so we meet none. Not even . . .

an ironic bow

. . . when "the Devil" comes to call beneath the elms. I bid you a good day.

Scratch: Good day to you, sir. Till we meet again.

Webster: That, I fear, will not be soon.

Scratch: Oh, do not fear. It will be very soon. Before the day ends.

Webster: Unhappily, you will not find me here this evening.

Scratch: I will not find you anywhere, Mr. Webster. *You* will find *me*.

Webster: Perhaps, but not *this* evening. My health was never better.

Scratch: You mistake me. I was not thinking of an . . . ultimate reunion — not for the moment anyway. I had in mind the next resumption of our little conversation. You interest me, Mr. Webster: more and more. I understand why, when you called on Mr. Jefferson at Monticello, he could not get enough of you. I quite believe it.

47

picking up his hat

But I trespass on your hospitality.

a bow: he prepares to leave the arbor — turns

Forgive me! One last question. You know Jabez
Stone?

Webster: Of Cross Corners? In New Hampshire? Certainly. Who doesn't?

Scratch: You think of Mr. Stone as an *American?*

Webster: American?

Scratch: You use the word as one of approbation — unusual approbation if you'll let me say so.

Webster: Then Jabez Stone deserves it. Youngest treasurer
the Party has ever had in New Hampshire or anywhere else in the Union.

Scratch: Done well, eh?

Webster: In politics, obviously. In business too: he's made
a fortune in the last ten years.

Scratch: Not *ten* years: seven, Mr. Webster — seven years
precisely lacking . . . just . . . one . . . day
. . . But I keep you from your numerous con-
cerns, your duties.

48

Webster: Worse, sir, you keep me from my sleep. When a
            man can't sleep beneath the noontime shadows
            of his garden elms without the insults of some
            passing mountebank he has no recourse but his
            bedroom sofa where he *can*.

            Webster stomps out.

Scratch: Then all's well. Bravo, Mr. Webster! Let's pre-
            serve the Union, keep the country going . . . get
            on with business.

The light fades. We are in:

SCENE THREE

Jabez Stone's farm at Cross Corners. Sunset. A hardscrabble, New England field. In the middle of the field, among the boulders and the steeple bush and milkweed, a rusted, one-horse plow lies on its side, its handles twisted against the light. Jabez, in his city clothes is standing staring at the plow, touching it. Scratch comes up behind him.

Scratch: Enjoying the sunset, Jabez? Charming moment! — that fiery light which leads us to the triumph of the dark . . . beautiful betrayal.

Jabez neither turns nor speaks.

                  Engrossed in it, eh? The hour of deception . . .

Jabez does not move.

                  And how appropriate! All that blazing red!

                  Couldn't keep away from the old plow, could you, Jabez? — not on what a man might call the . . . happy anniversary. Seven years ago today!

Silence, the reddening sky

                  Oh, come, my boy. It's not as bad as that. You've

had your seven years — and fat ones. Uninterrupted prosperity! Flowing affluence!

Jabez turns, looks Scratch in the eye.

That's better. Good evening, Jabez. How are you?

convulsion of silent laughter

Rarin' to go?

Jabez: *cool and collected*

I'm well. Quite well, thank you. What brings you here at this unusual hour?

Scratch: What's unusual about it? It happens every day along toward nightfall. Not always as beautiful as this, perhaps, but then not every nightfall is as promising — propitious.

Jabez: I hadn't thought of it in quite those terms.

Scratch: *gesture toward the plow*

But you *had* thought of it!

Jabez: I realized, of course, we had a settlement to make. As a matter of fact, I had it down on my calendar.

Scratch: Just so you wouldn't forget it in passing . . . With everything else you have to think about . . .

Jabez: The fact is, sir — I have no wish to sound inhos-
           pitable — the fact is that your call is rather pre-
           mature. It isn't *time*.

Scratch: You mean it isn't — shall we say — Eternity.
           You're right, of course — quite right. You're not
           . . . due till midnight.

He finds a seat on the stone wall.

           Eternity begins at twelve! How you will love
           Eternity, Jabez! No care for the morrow for there
           is no morrow. No regret for the vanished past for
           the past never vanishes: it floats along beside you
           on that ceaseless stream like a turd on a river.
           Whenever you look at it it's there, watching you,
           waiting to see what you decide to do about it . . .

stretching

           Except that there is nothing you *can* do about it.

a delicious noisy yawn

           Perfect peace! Perfect peace! I mean . . .

: pause

           . . . if only you could sleep it would be perfect.

pause

           But you can't sleep — not with your past beside
           you — floating there.

Jabez: *matter-of-fact*

> An inviting prospect but not, I fear, a prospect meant for me. Not this evening.

Scratch: *closing his eyes*

> Quite right. Not this evening. Not till midnight.

Jabez: And not at midnight either. I have important business in Concord in the morning.

Scratch: *a slight snore*

> It will have to wait . . .

deep sigh

> . . . indefinitely.

Jabez: *briskly, reaching into his pockets for papers — successful young executive in action*

> I do not propose that it shall wait, indefinitely or otherwise. The note may not be due till midnight but I shall meet it now — repay the loan at once.

Scratch: *opening his eyes*

> What note? What loan?

Jabez: The loan you so generously made me seven years ago. The note which undertook, upon a specified security, to repay that loan.

He is counting out banknotes as he talks: he now offers a little bundle.

> Please count them. You will see I have included interest to the hour specified.

Scratch has not moved.

> And may I take this opportunity to thank you once again for your great kindness to me. Without your generous advance of funds I never should have reached my present — shall I say — position. It was you, sir, who released my talents: talents of which I was quite ignorant until we met — until you offered me your helping hand.

Scratch: Keep your money *and* your gratitude, my friend. There *was* no loan: it was a purchase, a price paid. And what you call a note was not a note. It was a bill of sale promising delivery on a certain date and at a certain hour. And as for your sum total, do you really think my whole investment in this enterprise was those few, dog-eared, torn, devalued dollars? Who suggested you for treasurer of your party in this state? Who told the trustees of the Franklin Bank they needed a dirt farmer for their president? (You should have seen their faces when they found they *had* one!) No wonder you were ignorant of your talents, Jabez. They were never yours.

Jabez: Naturally if there are further services I should include I will be happy . . .

54

Scratch: Not services that cash could compensate. Men
             come to me . . .

making himself comfortable

> . . . men come to me as actors to the make-up
> table. In life as on the stage the face precedes the
> role and few men make their faces for themselves.
> One has to *live* to do that and living is too hard
> for most. They much prefer my pencil 'round the
> mouth and eyes and I provide it. For a compensa-
> tion. *Not* in cash. Oh, there are exceptions, cer-
> tainly. Take Daniel Webster. A wit in England
> says: "No man was ever great as Daniel Webster
> looks" — but Mr. Webster made his face himself
> . . . or . . . did he? That's the question isn't it?
> Well . . . we'll see.

silence: lost in thought

Jabez: Surely there must be some way we can estimate
             the total due . . .

Scratch: *his mind is elsewhere*

> There is. We have. You can deliver what you've
> promised on the stroke of twelve.

Jabez: I promised to repay a loan. I stand here ready to
             repay it.

Scratch: *himself again*

Did you? Let us consult the document.

He reaches into his inside coat pocket, pulls out the fat, yellow wallet, opens it: something small and fluttery and dark flies out. Scratch snatches at it and misses. We hear a small, high, squeaking voice which is nevertheless unmistakably human, unmistakably Yankee.

The Voice: Neighbor Stone! Neighbor Stone! Help me, help me, Neighbor Stone! For God's sake, help me!

Scratch whips out the red bandanna, catches the tiny creature with one fling, ties the ends around its leaping violence.

Jabez: *the businessman pose gone, his voice hoarse with terror*

That was a human voice! It called to me!

Scratch: *thumbing through a wad of papers*

I know. They always shout at first. Most embarrassing.

Jabez: But I *know* that voice!

Scratch: *reading*

Scoville, Sherwin, Slater, Stevens . . .

Jabez: Stevens! Miser Stevens! That was Miser Stevens's voice! I'd know it anywhere — that whine.

56

Scratch: *Here* we are: *Stone.* Everything shipshape and apple pie.

He unfolds a document and begins to read:

"I, Jabez Stone, of Cross Corners . . ."

Jabez: I tell you that was Miser Stevens's voice and it must be Miser Stevens in your red bandanna and Miser Stevens isn't even . . . dead!

Scratch: *clearing his throat menacingly*

"I, Jabez Stone . . ."

Jabez: You can't tell me he's dead. He was just as spry and mean as a woodchuck Tuesday and here it is . . .

Scratch: *the familiar smile*

Ah, Jabez, we don't know, do we? We never know. In the midst of life we are in . . .

The tolling of a bell somewhere off across the valley

Listen!

First Church I'd say by the sound of it. They bought a used bell from Second Church and it turned out just a leetle cracked. The Congregation at Second Church had never even noticed — so they said. Interdenominational differences, I suppose.

57

Jabez: First Church is Miser Stevens's!

Scratch: It . . .

*A high, fierce, twanging whine from the bandanna: the little crea-
ture beating like a June bug against a screen. Jabez is staring at it,
his face twisted with horror.*

              . . . *was!*

Jabez: Are they all as . . . small as that?

Scratch: As him? Oh, no. They vary. You'll run fair to
              middling, Jabez. It's hard to judge precisely in
              . . . advance. Except, of course, in special cases.
              I mentioned Daniel Webster. You'd know before
              you measured with a man like that. The head
              alone! Spectacular. Nothing like it since Ben-
              jamin Franklin . . . and he eluded me . . .
              Pity!

        pause

              Well, shall we get on? "I, Jabez Stone of Cross
              Corners . . ."

Jabez: *collapsing*

              No need to read it. It's a bill of sale. Delivery at
              midnight. I know every word of it by heart.

        grasping at Scratch

Please! Give me one more year! Just one!

Scratch: We'll make it easy for you, Jabez . . . easy as we can.

He reaches out, touches Jabez's head with his hand, arranges his hair, appraises the effect like a mortician preparing a corpse.

Jabez: I don't want it easy. I just want one more . . .

Scratch: I know. I know. But that's not possible, is it, Jabez? We have a contract, haven't we? — a bill of sale? — a very comprehensive bill of sale if I do say so: I drafted it myself.

Jabez: *a revulsion of desperate rage*

Then I'll break it! I'll get a lawyer and I'll break it. There never was a contract drawn a lawyer couldn't break.

Scratch: *Get* a lawyer: you've *got* one — two, as a matter of fact.

meditatively

I grant they could be better.

Jabez: I'll get the best. I'll get . . . Daniel Webster! I'm the Treasurer of the Party in this State. I have friends. All I have to do is send for him — he'll come.

59

Scratch:	Daniel *Webster!*
Jabez:	He knows me. Everybody in New Hampshire knows me and Daniel Webster is New Hampshire born. He knew my father. Knew my grandfather.
Scratch:	But Daniel Webster is now *Secretary.* Secretary of State to Mr. Fillmore!
Jabez:	He's my friend.
Scratch:	Really? Drop the cares of State for friendship?
Jabez:	Friendship and a fee. He's always short of cash.
Scratch:	Whereas — how fortunate! — you're not.
Jabez:	He knows I'm good for anything he asks.
Scratch:	I'm sure he does. But if he's down in Washington . . .
Jabez:	He isn't. He's next door in Massachusetts.
Scratch:	Extraordinary! *All* you have to do is send?

He studies the fading sky, color of rusty blood. Jabez, turning with him, stares not at the sky but the plow.

Getting a little darker, isn't it? I see you're looking at the old plow, Jabez. Sort of brings things back . . . ?

Yep, it's getting darker. Hear those crickets? Regular kind of clock-tick, isn't it? That's what they're doing maybe — counting time — counting the running out of time. Listen to them, Jabez!

Silence. We listen to the crickets — the mechanical insistent beat. Jabez on his knees at Scratch's feet

Jabez: No, no. I didn't mean it. I won't break the contract — try to. I won't send for anyone if you'll just help me. One more year, one more.

 speechless — huddled on the ground

 Oh, dear God, don't . . . don't . . .

Silence — the crickets — Scratch touches Jabez's head, strokes it, jerks it brutally back.

Scratch: Maybe you had better send for Mr. Webster, Jabez.

Jabez sags in the dwindling light. The beat of the crickets is louder and louder.

CURTAIN

SCENE FOUR

Jabez's farm at Cross Corners. Night. The interior of the old barn. A lighted lantern on a nail: another farther back. A few chairs. A table. Webster, carpetbag in hand, enters.

Webster: Jabez!

Jabez gets up from a dark corner.

Jabez: Mr. Webster . . . Thank God, you're here. Thank God.

Webster: *looking up and around at the huge beams, the high roof*

Your driver, that venerable First Selectman, Mr. Josiah Salter, *told* me I'd find you in the barn . . .

putting down his gear

. . . and here, by Goshas, in the barn you be! What is it, Neighbor Stone?

Jabez: You mean . . . the barn? I thought we'd be more comfortable here. Wives get nervous when they see a lawyer in the house. Particularly, sir, a famous lawyer.

Webster: And more particularly, Mr. Stone, when they see a lawyer after lawyers' hours — famous or not. What's wrong? Mutiny among the Whigs? Embezzlement at Franklin Savings?

Jabez: Oh, nothing like that, sir.

Webster: Well, if it's not the bank and not the party, what *is* wrong?

His voice has an edge.

Somebody shoot your dog?

Jabez: No, no.

Webster: Well, then, what did happen?

The door creaks: Jabez whirls to face it.

Expecting somebody?

Jabez is silent, motionless facing the door.

All right. Don't talk till you're a mind to.
Maybe something . . . potable would help.

No answer

Latin *potabilis* — from *potare* — to *drink*.

Jabez turns, his face blank.

> Not to put too fine a point upon it, Cross Corners applejack is famous.

Jabez: Ah, yes, forgive me . . .

> *He scrambles up a ladder to the hayloft.*

Webster: Might even help remind you why you sent for me to come.

Jabez is back with the jug.

> Sit down, boy, sit down.

> I remember one chill summer evening almost forty years ago, your grandfather fetched me up a jug of his eighteen-ten . . .

Jabez hands him the jug and a dingy glass.

> I've never learned to drink alone, not even in Washington — and in Washington you sometimes have to drink alone . . . if you want a gentleman for company. You take the mug, I'll take the jug. Your health, sir.

> *A gulp from the jug skillfully balanced on the back of his elbow.*

> Well?

Jabez, head down over his glass

Take your time, boy. Take your time.

another long pull

> I remember teaching your grandfather a bit of doggerel that evening. He did not, under ordinary circumstances, care for song, but a pull or two at the eighteen-ten would make a thrush of anybody.
>
> It went like this:

He throws his head back, emitting a deep tuneless basso profundo: he is tone deaf.

> "When you and I are dead and gone . . ."

Jabez gags, coughs.

> Hold on, boy! You have to hold hard when the applejack jerks at you. So . . .

refilling Jabez's glass, a long quaff

> "When you and I are dead and gone
> This busy world will still jog on . . ."
>
> What's the matter, boy? Ill? You look . . .
>
> What *is* it, Jabez? Why *did* you send for me?
>
> At *midnight!*

Jabez: I'm sorry. I had no choice . . .

Webster: No, no. I was happy to come — happy to come

. . . and not for your grandfather's sake or your father's, but for yours. We respect and admire you, all of us in New England — even the Democrats. But *twelve midnight!* What kind of lawyer's business falls upon that hour?

Jabez: A . . .

floundering

. . . mortgage case.

Webster: *Mortgage* case! *Foreclosure* you mean? At *midnight?*

Jabez: Foreclosed.

Webster: Not the home farm certainly.

Jabez: The home farm . . .

He looks around him at the table, the chairs, the old furniture, as though he were seeing them for the first time — or the last

Webster: Come, come, Jabez. You're one of the richest men in the state — the richest maybe west of Portsmouth and Portsmouth smells the sea. Pull yourself together, Jabez.

Jabez: I'm no lawyer, Mr. Webster. All I know is . . . well, I've lost . . . everything.

66

Webster: Listen to me, Jabez. What's all this about? Begin at the beginning.

Jabez: That was seven years ago . . .

pause

Webster: Go on.

Jabez: Oh, Mr. Webster, I never should have sent for you. I can't tell *you.* My grandfather — well, he loved you, Mr. Webster. My father honored you. All New England, all the Union, honors you. You are the Defender of the Union, the Expounder of the Constitution . . .

Webster: I'm afraid you'll *have* to tell me, Jabez. Not that I don't appreciate the sentiments . . .

reaching for the jug

What happened seven years ago?

Jabez: I was plowing. It was a hot day in a dry summer and the hay was in — what hay there was that year. I was planning on winter wheat — had to have a cash crop somehow with the children sick, first one child then another, and my wife as crooked as a scythe snath with the rheumatism. I hadn't paid the doctor for a year or anyone else but the tax collector and I was late with him. So I was plowing — the only piece on the farm you *can* plow — the water mowing where the brook comes in. You have to watch for boulders in that meadow and I was watching, thinking of all the times I'd plowed the piece before and the times my father had plowed it and his father and all at once — well, you can guess. We fetched up on a granite boulder must have heaved with the frost in the big freeze that winter and the colter broke and the old horse foundered and . . .

his voice goes dry in his throat

Well, I suppose I kind of . . .

his voice trails off unconvincingly

. . . cursed . . .

Webster: *a bark of a laugh*

Who wouldn't!

Jabez:
Except that there was someone passing. I could have sworn he wasn't there before and you can see the road for a mile from the water mowing. A Boston-looking man in a neat red buggy.

He dropped the reins and jumped the wall as though I'd called him. Exactly as though he'd heard me call him. I remember thinking he was mighty spry for a Boston man and then before I knew it he was there — talking to me. Don't ask me what he said. All I know is, it was like a revelation.

You know how it is when you hear a song and you can't remember the words but the moment stays with you, haunts you — changes your life? I can't remember the words. He took it all in, the broken colter, the stranded plow, the foundered horse, the boulders around in the grass like grave-stones, the crooked house, the barn blown in at the north end, the hills beyond it — ridge on ridge of wooded hills — and he wanted to know how a man could live like that when there were towns to live in, houses with water laid on by the kitchen sink and coal to heat with, and all the rest of it.

You see, I'd always thought a man did what he had to: stayed put and did what he had to. That's the way they brought us up. You did what you had to, best you could. If the work was hard it was your work. It never crossed my mind a man could leave — clear out — live as he wanted to. But here was this Boston man by the broken plow at the furrow's end in the hardscrabble meadow telling me I could do just that. It was what I say — a revelation. I saw what a fool I'd been!

a harsh laugh that ends like a sob

. . . been! . . .

pause

He offered to help. Said he'd be back at midnight. With a kind of — advance, you might say.

69

Webster: And you signed a note for it? — a mortgage note,
            I think you told me.

Jabez nods.

            Payable in . . . . ?

Jabez: Seven years: midnight to midnight.

Webster: And the seven years are up . . . ?

Jabez: Tonight. At midnight . . . *Now!*
            O, my God!

Webster: *cheerfully*

            Well, we'll have to ask for an extension.

Jabez: You don't understand, Mr. Webster.

Webster: What don't I understand?

Scratch appears behind them unseen by either.

            I understand mortgages. This isn't the first fore-
            closure in New Hampshire or even the first in my
            practice at the bar.

Scratch: *taps Webster on the shoulder, a wheeze of rusty laughter*

            He's right, Mr. Webster. You *don't* understand.

Webster: *wheeling, exploding*

        Oh, Great God in Heaven!

Scratch: No, no. You mistake me, Mr. Webster.

Webster: On the contrary. I know now how you make your living. You run a mortgage business . . .

      Exaggerated irony

        . . . on the side.

Scratch: A mortgage business, Mr. Webster?

      a quick look at Jabez

      Ah, of course, a mortgage business! In any case we meet again: I think I . . . prophesied we would. The greatest possible pleasure, Mr. Webster.

Webster: Sit down, will you?

Scratch: *He picks up the jug, shakes it, blows his nose with a resounding ironic blast, sits down.*

      I am obliged to you for your presence, Mr. Webster. It will simplify a sometimes embarrassing transaction.

Webster: Embarrassing transaction? An attempted foreclosure of a mortgage is . . . embarrassing?

Scratch: Ah, you *will* have your little pleasantries, Mr.
              Webster.

Webster: You deny you are here to foreclose a mortgage?

Scratch: Not if you prefer the phrase.

   a lip-licking grin at Jabez

              Not in the least. Anything he has a mind to call
              it as long as I get my rights and judgment is . . .

   lingering pleasantly over the word

                 . . . ex-e-cuted.

Jabez huddles into his chair.

Webster: May I take that to mean you *have* a judgment?

Scratch: Judgment?

Webster: An adjudication. By a court. Of competent juris-
              diction. Finding the note due, valid, and unpaid.
              Ordering execution on the property.

Scratch: *savoring the word with a pull at the jug*

                 "The *property*"!

   gagging over the drink

Your client, Mr. Webster, should be indicted for his liquor before he is sued for his . . . debt!

Webster: Have you, or have you not, an adjudication by a court . . .

Scratch: . . . of competent jurisdiction? The elegance of your phrases, Mr. Webster! I have.

Webster: May I see it?

Scratch: Better than that you may hear it. I, Mr. Webster, am the Court of Competent Jurisdiction. I will rule . . .

Webster: You will not, sir! Not in Cross Corners in New Hampshire in the United States of America. In the United States of America a litigant does not sit in judgment. Under the Constitution of the United States . . .

Scratch: You and your Constitution, Mr. Webster! You'll be telling me next your Constitution has supplanted the laws of the universe and your people are not as other people.

Webster: It has and they're not. They're a new thing under the sun. They're Americans!

Scratch: New?

a contemptuous look at Jabez

73

Like your client? I can remember a time when the new thing under the sun on this continent was the red man and his bow. The world was much the same then only . . . nobody had thought to call it new. A restful moment! Well . . . that's gone . . . And so you want a judge and jury?

Webster: Not in the least. *You* want a judge and jury.

Scratch: And *I* won't do.

Webster: *You* won't do. No offense intended.

Scratch: And none taken.

rubbing his chin, looking away as a cat looks away from the mouse under her claws

But where in the world will I find a judge and jury at this place and hour?

Webster: That, I fear, is your responsibility.

Scratch: *just a shade too quickly*

My responsibility?

Webster: You're the one who needs them.

Scratch: How cogently you put things, Mr. Webster. So . . . you leave it to me.

Webster: If you'll leave it to *them*. *After* they've heard the evidence, of course, and the arguments of counsel.

Scratch: Above all . . .

an ironic bow

. . . the arguments of counsel. So any judge and jury I may find at this unlikely hour on this forsaken hill will satisfy you.

Webster: Any *American* judge and jury.

Scratch: And that is your one condition? Any American judge. Any American jury.

Webster: Precisely.

Scratch: Then you shall have them, sir. *Precisely!*

He stamps his foot. A throng of white-faced, ghastly figures in the dress of other centuries appear from all corners of the barn. Jabez shrivels in his chair. Scratch turns to Webster.

Your judge, sir, and your jury!

Scratch grins at Webster — a long, slow, unsmiling, widening grin.

Well . . . ?

Silence

You see how it is, Mr. Webster.

Webster: *looking him full in the face, shoulders set, feet firm*

How it is, and *who*.

Scratch: Not just the Old Scratch any longer, eh? — not
a laughable way of mentioning what no one men-
tions laughing.

pause

I thought you'd recognize me once the light was
right — even in General Washington's Republic.

Webster: *looking at the jury man by man: a silence we can feel
— taste almost*

I owe you . . . apology would be an inappropri-
ate word but . . .

Scratch: I repeat: Your judge and jury!

Webster: *facing them again*

Not mine. I made, and you accepted, a condition.

Scratch: *Condition?*

Webster: That judge and jury be American.

Scratch: *contemptuously*

American!

They are: you have my word for it.

Webster: *They!*

Scratch: Nothing, sir, was said of *live* Americans.

a long silence

This, sir, is Mr. Justice Hathorne, an American jurist. The best remembered — longest anyway — of all American jurists. He presided at certain famous trials in the Massachusetts city of Salem where a number of women — as you, of course, remember — were convicted of . . . witchcraft. They were hanged. No judge, you will agree, was ever more American than Mr. Justice Hathorne. Salem . . . the Old Colony . . .

Hathorne stands aside.

Burr!

A small, dapper man in Continental uniform advances, a huge dueling pistol in his hand.

And this is Colonel Aaron Burr. Once Vice-President of the United States and . . .

a glance at Webster

all but President. He was indicted for treason later on but not convicted: he claimed he had merely intended to make a revolution in *Mex-*

ico! I think you'll agree that a Vice-President of the United States qualifies as an *American!* It is true, of course, that Colonel Burr thought best to leave the country for a number of years but he returned — he returned.

Burr climbs the ladder to the hayloft.

De Wolf!

A tall handsome man in the dress of a Yankee Captain of the 1790s advances.

Here we have Captain James De Wolf of Rhode Island, the most famous slave trader of a state famous for its trade in slaves. Captain Jim, as he was affectionately called, was a most enterprising American. He was elected United States Senator toward the end of his life but disliked the Washington climate and resigned.

De Wolf joins Burr in the loft.

Lynch!

A white-faced planter of the 1770s steps forward.

This is Charles Lynch of Virginia whose activities as a justice of the peace in that state added a famous word to your interesting vocabulary. Judge Lynch's credentials as an American are impeccable — a soldier — a patriot. If he sometimes seemed a little too enthusiastic in his sentencing

78

of prisoners, his purposes were admirable. The Virginia Assembly, in exonerating him after the Revolution, specifically stated that his judgments, though not "strictly warranted by law," were "justifiable" because they maintained order in a dangerous time. What could be more fundamentally American than *that?*

Lynch joins Burr and De Wolf.

And now! *Now!* Dr. Benjamin Church of Massachusetts . . .

A tall, handsomely dressed eighteenth-century doctor advances.

the first and only member of the Revolutionary apparatus in America to have his family pensioned after his death by the British Crown! Doctor Church, gentlemen, was the first American traitor!

As Dr. Church follows Lynch up the ladder, a figure in seventeenth-century dress with blue jowl, smirking mouth and piously folded hands moves forward.

Oh, no! No! There must have been some misunderstanding. *This* is Mr. John Webb of Massachusetts Bay who led the Quaker woman, Mary Dyer, out onto Boston Common to be hanged on a damp morning in 1660. But of course Mr. Webb was not alone. They were all there from the governor down. And they *did* establish a great American tradition: how to deal with dis-

79

senting opinions. Nevertheless . . . one has to draw the line at some point. Well, since you're here, Mr. Webb, up with you!

As Webb climbs, the rest of the jurors crowd forward. Scratch motions them up the ladder.

Come along! Up with you! This is a distinguished New Yorker, Captain Kidd. A colleague of his from Ocracoke Island in North Carolina. An empire-builder from the Northwest Territories — what he couldn't cut or saw he burned. A Revolutionary officer who plotted against General Washington. *Nothing* is more American than service in the Revolutionary Army, is it? Ask the daughters and the daughters' daughters and on down . . .

Well, Mr. Webster, are you satisfied?

Silence

I asked you: are you satisfied with judge and jury?

Webster: A judge and jury of the dead and damned . . .

Scratch: *American* dead and damned!

Webster: . . . to try an action for *foreclosure?*

Scratch: That, I think, was *your* term, Mr. Webster.

Silence

Well . . . We wait on you, sir. Are you ready to proceed?

A long silence

Webster: Defendant . . . is ready to proceed.

Scratch: Oyez! Oyez! Oyez! The Honorable, the Inferior Court of Common Pleas in the County of Oyez! Oyez! Oyez!

Hathorne enters the old chaise, raps with a makeshift gavel.

Hathorne: The Court will be in order.

Scratch: *rising, bowing to the Court, bowing to the jury, bowing to Webster*

> May it please the Court. This is an action on a debt — not quite the usual debt but an obligation notwithstanding — alleged by the plaintiff . . .

indicating himself with a modest gesture

> . . . to have been executed by the defendant . . .

a bow in the direction of Jabez Stone

> on the twenty-sixth day of July, eighteen hundred and forty-three, being due and, so to speak, payable to the plaintiff seven years from date on the twenty-sixth day of July in the year eighteen hun-

dred and fifty which is the day just now, with the passage of midnight . . .

a vicious sting in his voice

concluded!

Hathorne: You may proceed.

Scratch: Plaintiff in this action is represented by himself. Defendant is represented by the Honorable Daniel Webster . . . Secretary of State of the so-called United States of America. The Secretary takes a serious view of this litigation. He considers that the vital interests of what he likes to call the Union are involved, and nothing — neither time nor space nor bad roads nor unreasonable hours — has prevented his presence.

Webster: If the Court please!

Hathorne: The Court will hear you.

Webster: There is no need for irrelevant and insulting innuendoes touching the integrity of the Republic in an action for debt, nor, indeed, in any other action. The Union stands. It will continue to stand. Nothing — not all the evil of the world — can prevent its standing.

Scratch: But, of course. Of course. I quite agree. Nothing can destroy the Union — not even what dis-

82

tinguished counsel eloquently calls the Evil of the
World — nothing at all . . .

dropping his voice almost to a whisper

> . . . except the Union! When the Union has *it-
> self* become an evil . . .

pause

> But counsel for the defendant is quite right, quite
> right. As befits the greatest constitutional lawyer
> of this or any other age, he believes in institutions
> — particularly the institutions which compose his
> Union. He regards them as the wonders of the
> world to be preserved at any cost — particularly
> at any moral cost . . .

Webster: Your Honor, I protest this . . .

Scratch: Not in the least. Not in the least. I intend noth-
              ing offensive, nothing whatever. Moral costs are
              the most easily paid of any. A few tears, a few
              eloquent and appropriate regrets will do it. In-
              stitutions are real. Moral twinges are — what?
              Moral twinges!

Webster: May it please the Court . . .

Hathorne: Come to your point, sir.

Webster: May it please the Court, this is an action for debt

— an action for the collection of an alleged debt. The United States of America are not on trial.

Scratch: Can we be sure, Mr. Webster? Can we be sure? You recall your extravagant admiration for your fellow Americans — your belief that no American owes allegiance to a certain . . . power you were kind enough to name. Suppose we should discover there was one respected American who was capable of precisely that. Would we not be entitled to assume there might be others, equally respected, or even more so, who were equally capable? And if others why not many others? Why not all? Why not your *Union?*

Webster: *If* the Court please . . .

Scratch: Why not, indeed, that great defender of the Union who would put the Union first before everything, even its promises, even the most solemn of its promises — that great defender of the Union who has the courage and the honesty to call the Union what it is?

Webster: *the full resounding resonance of his tremendous voice*

If it please the Court . . .

Scratch: I will not persist. I will not persist. I merely wanted my respect for moral twinges on the record.

Hathorne: *bang of the gavel*

Proceed!

Scratch: Very well, Your Honor. I face however a proce-
             dural difficulty at the outset. I wish to put the
             plaintiff on the stand. Which means that I must,
             so to speak, put myself on the stand as witness
             and question myself in my capacity as counsel.

Webster: I have no objection, Your Honor.

Hathorne: Defendant has no objection.

Scratch: Thank you, sir. I speak then as counsel address-
             ing myself as witness. Do you recognize the pa-
             per . . .

He draws a folded paper from his pocket.

             . . . I now hand you? I reply in my capacity as
             witness . . .

Webster: One moment, Your Honor. This witness has not
             been sworn.

Scratch: This witness, may it please the Court, cannot be
             sworn — has reasons of . . . conscience for de-
             clining to be sworn.

Webster: No evidence may be received in any American
             court unless the witness has been sworn to tell
             the truth, the whole truth and nothing but the
             truth . . .

Hathorne: Proceed!

Webster: I object.

Hathorne: Objection overruled.

Webster: I must respectfully persist in my objection. No
             evidence may be received in any American
             court . . .

Bang of the gavel

Hathorne: You cannot persist in an objection after the ob-
             jection has been overruled. You are in contempt
             of this court.

Scratch: *mildly*

             May the witness now reply to the question?

Hathorne: Answer the question.

Scratch: Do you recognize the paper in your hand?

Scratch: I do.

Scratch: Describe it.

Scratch: It is an instrument executed by the defendant,
             Jabez Stone, and given me by him seven years
             ago . . .

     pause

. . . yesterday.

Scratch: How is this instrument signed?

Scratch: Jabez Stone.

Scratch: May it please the Court, the plaintiff submits this document thus described and authenticated as Exhibit A.

Hathorne: The document will be marked Plaintiff's Exhibit A.

Webster: I object.

Hathorne: Objection overruled.

Webster: This, Your Honor, is a travesty of justice. You have admitted into evidence the unsworn testimony of a witness who is also a party to this litigation. You have overruled my objection to the admission of this unsworn testimony and have threatened me with punishment for persisting in the assertion of my client's most elementary rights. You are now offered an exhibit based upon this inadmissible evidence . . .

Scratch: May it please the Court, I think perhaps I can suggest a means of satisfying the earnest protests of counsel for the defendant, while saving the Court's time and protecting the interests of that perfect justice for which Your Honor is revered.

Hathorne:	The Court will hear you.
Scratch:	There is present in the courtroom, and immediately available, a witness who can identify this document and who will have no slightest objection to being sworn — who will, indeed, expect it. I refer, of course, to the defendant.
Hathorne:	Let the defendant take the stand.

Jabez, stumbling, comes forward.

	Raise your right hand. Repeat after me. I do solemnly swear . . .
Jabez:	I do solemnly swear . . .
Hathorne:	That the testimony I am about to give . . .
Jabez:	That the testimony I am about to give . . .
Hathorne:	Will be the truth, the whole truth and nothing but the truth . . .
Jabez:	. . . nothing but the truth . . .

So help me . . .

God.

Scratch:	Your name?
Jabez:	Jabez Stone.

Scratch: Residence?

Jabez: Cross Corners in the state of New Hampshire.

Scratch: Occupation?

Jabez: Farmer.

Scratch: *Occupation?*

Jabez: Banker. Landed proprietor. Treasurer of the
              Whig Party in the state of New Hampshire . . .

   defiantly

              . . . farmer.

Scratch: *turning to watch Webster*

              You are an American?

Jabez: I am.

Scratch: Your father was an American?

Jabez: *a note of pride*

              He was.

Scratch: And his father?

Jabez: His father.

Scratch: And his?

Jabez: His.

Scratch: I congratulate you, Mr. Webster.

Now, Mr. Jabez Stone of Cross Corners in the state of New Hampshire, banker, landed proprietor, treasurer of the Whig Party, American and descendant of Americans, I show you a document marked Plaintiff's Exhibit A. I ask you if you have seen this document before.

Jabez: *a piteous look at Webster*

I have.

Scratch: I direct your attention to the signature at the foot of this document. Do you recognize this signature?

Jabez: I do.

Scratch: Whose signature is it?

Silence, Jabez covering his mouth with his hand

Whose signature is it, Mr. Jabez Stone?

Jabez: *barely audible*

My signature.

Scratch: *pleasantly*

Y*our* signature. And in what — ah — medium is this signature of yours inscribed?

No answer

I ask you, Mr. Jabez Stone, in what medium this signature you recognize as yours is written.

No answer: the jury, stirring, craning

Would you say ink, sir?

No answer

Not ink. In what then?

Jabez: *very quietly*

Blood.

Scratch: I did not catch your answer, Mr. Stone.

Jabez: Blood.

Scratch: Very well, Mr. Jabez Stone. You have recognized the document marked Plaintiff's Exhibit A. You have testified that the signature is yours. Will you now read it to the jury.

Jabez: I, Jabez Stone of Cross Corners in the state of New Hampshire, having received and acknowledged an irrevocable promise to supply me with all the amenities, comforts and gratifications of

91

life throughout a period of seven years of uninterrupted prosperity and continuing affluence, do
hereby undertake and agree to deliver . . .

. . . at the close of business

. . . being the hour of midnight

. . . on the last day of the said seventh

year . . .

His head down: silence

. . . my immortal soul.

*Silence. Webster staring at Jabez, rising, moving slowly toward
him across the barn, Scratch sidling along behind him*

Webster: Your . . . *what?*

Scratch: *whisper*

. . . his immortal soul . . .

*Wheeze of laughter, the jury sniggering, cackling, shrieking in
derision, a mounting, swelling chaos of jeering sound*

That, Mr. Webster, is your "mortgage" . . .
your "foreclosure"? . . . Do you want a "judgment," too?

pause

On whom? Him?

Silence

> Or on your country? — on your bright new world — which bore him and bears hundreds like him every day?
>
> Not your country?
>
> Then, perhaps, that great defender of your country who defends now . . .

contemptuously

> *Jabez Stone!*

Silence: the restless jury. Then Jabez's frightened, stammering voice

Jabez: Mr. Webster . . .

           If it please the . . .

                       may I consult my . . .

Scratch: Defendant wishes to consult his lawyer. Maybe his lawyer should consult one, too.

Hathorne: The Court will be in brief recess.

Jabez, down from the stand, stumbles across the barn to Webster, huddles beside him.

Jabez: You see . . . how it is.

Webster: *How* it is. And *who* it is. *And* what he wants here.

93

Jabez:	I'm not worth . . . throw the case up, Mr. Webster! Let him take me!
Webster:	Take *you!* He's after bigger game. You're nothing but the fish head in the mink trap, Neighbor Stone!
Jabez:	I know. I know now. He wants *you.*
Webster:	More than me. If he can shame the country with your shame he'll *take* the country — make a butt and byword of our talk of human decency, of human worth — make fools of all of us.
Jabez:	You must believe me, Mr. Webster, I never thought . . . I never meant to get you into . . . I was . . . *frightened!*

his face in his hands

Webster:	Nothing to be ashamed of, Jabez. I'm frightened too. Oh, not the fear of dying: I'm too old for that . . . too close to it. No, the fear of losing everything I've loved and lived for — my whole life — my life's whole work — the Union . . . the Republic.

Silence, the jurors creeping from their loft, listening, creeping nearer, listening

I've always known — we all do — that there's evil in the universe. Purposeful evil. Not the opposite of good or the defect of good but some-

94

thing to which good itself is an irrelevance, a fantasy — the wish for darkness underneath the love of light. I know that, Jabez. But to meet it face to face — the contemptuous derisive laughter! To learn that what it laughs at is mankind — man's life — man's hope of life!

pause

No, Jabez, I won't pretend that I'm not frightened.

Jabez: Oh, Mr. Webster, go while you still can.

Webster: And leave that hope to him! No, there's only one way now to save what he's determined to destroy.

a long pause

Ever meet Seth Peterson down at Marshfield? Hired man? He'd tell you: he tells me! Count by men, he says, and shame the Devil. He means the man comes first — whatever man — the last — the least — *because* he's last and least. He means the way to save the country is to save the man.

pause

He's right. I guess there never was another way.

pause

You may be nothing much to brag of, Jabez, but you're here. By God, I'll save you.

Jabez: You can't, Mr. Webster. There's no defense.

Webster: I'll be damned from Hell to breakfast if two Americans can't find a way to beat the Devil.

Scratch: *a chuckle*

Truer words were never spoken, Mr. Webster.

Hathorne: The Court will be in . . .

Scratch: *Crash of the jug on the table: his voice brutal*

No! That game is over. I'll write the rules now and I'll take . . .

off across the barn floor like a hawk in a hen yard

. . . what's mine.

He has Jabez by the scruff of the neck, Webster on his feet

Webster: Not yours until you've won your verdict.

Scratch: Nonsense! *I'll* give the verdicts.

Webster: You made yourself a party to this litigation. You gave me your assurance that the jury would decide — and only after it had heard the evidence . . .

Scratch: You have no evidence!

Webster: . . . and heard the arguments . . .

Scratch: There is no argument. Nothing whatever is in issue now. I *have* him. If this jury brought its verdict in for me — as it would bring it — what would I have then more than I have now?

He jerks Jabez up by the collar as a hunter lifts the body of his fox.

Webster: If the jury found for you you'd have the scalp of Daniel Webster.

Scratch: Ah?

He drops Jabez, turns to Webster: the old, ironic, genial tone.

And by the scalp you mean . . . the man?

Webster: The Indians thought so.

Scratch: So then we understand each other. If the trial goes on, something — perhaps we might say, Mr. Webster's scalp — even *Mr. Webster* — will be at stake?

Webster: *long pause*

Yes.

They shake hands.

Scratch: Oh, Mr. Webster!

    his cat-canary smile

        Why then we will . . . proceed.

Webster: *full voice, pushing Jabez forward*

        Witness will resume the stand.

Scratch: Thank you, Mr. Webster, but we've finished with this witness.

Webster: I have the right, I think, to cross-examine.

Scratch: Cross-examine! He's your client.

Webster: My client but your witness: you put him on the stand.

Scratch: *giving up*

        Witness will resume the stand.

Bang of the gavel

Webster: Now, Mr. Stone, you have testified that you signed the instrument here in evidence.

Jabez: I so testified.

Webster: That you signed it in blood.

Jabez: I did.

Webster: In your own blood.

Jabez: In my own blood.

Webster: You read the document to the jury.

Jabez: I did.

Webster: Did you read it truly?

Jabez: I did. Truly.

Webster: It is true, then, that this document is in effect a bill of sale of your immortal soul? — *your soul* for seven years of affluence — of comfort — gratification, I think the word was?

Jabez: *faltering*

             It it true.

Webster: Now, Mr. Stone, when you retained me to represent you in this litigation did you or did you not inform me of the true nature of this document?

The jury leans forward listening. Even Hathorne is listening. Scratch has his back to the scene as though it didn't matter.

Jabez: *an anguished look at Webster: he still trusts him but . . .*

99

I did not.

Webster: On the contrary, you misled me.

Jabez: I misled you.

Webster: You permitted me to believe that you required
             my services in connection with the foreclosure of
             a mortgage?

Jabez: I did.

Webster: In brief . . . you lied to me.

Jabez: *his eyes fixed piteously on Webster: he doesn't understand*

             I lied to you.

Webster: Very well, Mr. Stone. Let us now have the truth,
             the whole truth and nothing but the truth, so
             help you . . .

         The word is like the thud of an ax

             . . . God!

             Why did you lie to me?

Jabez: I was ashamed of the . . . truth.

Webster: Of having signed that . . . bill of sale?

Jabez: Of having signed it.

Webster: Then why *did* you sign it?

Jabez: *in anguish*

Because I couldn't bear my . . . life.

Webster: *What* life?

Jabez: The broken plow. The foundered horse. The farm. Those terrible unending winters, treacherous springs, the loneliness at dusk, the wind at night . . . my wife a girl still and grown old — my children sick or dead beneath those gravestones in the meadow. The farm. I couldn't bear it.

Webster: Your father bore it.

Scratch: Really, Your Honor. I object. Why does it matter what this witness *feels?* It is totally and eternally immaterial whether Mr. Jabez Stone can bear his life. His death either.

Webster: *to Hathorne*

Immaterial perhaps to counsel for the plaintiff, but not, Your Honor, to a Court which knows as you do what it is to live and die.

Silence — Webster and Hathorne eye to eye

Hathorne: *as though to himself*

Objection overruled.

Scratch stands staring at Hathorne.

Webster: Your father bore it, Mr. Stone. Raised four children out of nine. Educated two of them.

brutally

They bore it . . . but you couldn't?

Jabez: I couldn't.

Webster: You *couldn't!* So you sold your soul for a mess of
. . . gratifications!

A *long pause: Webster staring at Jabez Stone, a curt,
over-the-shoulder word to Scratch.*

Your witness.

Scratch: No questions. He admits the transaction. Con-
firms the . . . debt is due and payable.

Webster: Due, yes. Payable is for the jury.

Scratch: What do you mean? You yourself have told your
client that he sold his soul . . . Something, you
once believed, that no *American* would do!

Webster: Something one American, alas, has done.

Scratch: *One* American! Multitudes of them. Multitudes!
There was even one who sold his *country's* soul!

Ever hear of that one, Mr. Webster? Sold it for
peace, he said . . . to preserve the Union! Took
back his country's promise to mankind for a few

years' peace — for a spell of prosperity. *You* remember that one, don't you?

Oh, to be sure, it was a childish promise, a ridiculous promise, the kind of promise men believed in back in those American woods — rattle of idiot words like sleet on the oak leaves — like gabble of geese in the autumn sky — like a loon on a lake.

All men had a right to Liberty!

Men!

Liberty!

Anyway you took it back. You were an honest man and sensible and you took it back.

All men had a right to Liberty, yes, but if a *black* man tried to use it he was still a slave — worse than a slave — a *fugitive slave.* You returned him to . . . *servitude.*

It was all in the Constitution, you said, and besides, it would keep the peace, preserve the Union.

That was what you told the country, Mr. Webster, and it worked. It preserved the Union . . .

. . . for a little . . .

pause

Nevertheless, there was one American who sold his country's soul.

I wonder, Mr. Webster, if you think he sold his own? We'd welcome him if he did.

103

to the jury

> Wouldn't we, gentlemen?

pause

> I didn't catch your answer, Mr. Webster. *Did* he sell his soul?

Silence

> Or is *that* what you mean? — is *that*, perhaps, the question for the jury?

The jury gathering silently around Webster — a long silence

Webster: The question for the jury, sir?

The question for the jury?

The question for the jury is what it always has been from the first beginnings of the dream of human justice.

The question for the jury is the question of imperfect man: whether a man must perish because he has deserved to perish . . .

Whether a nation, because it has deserved to fall, must fall.

Whether fallible, imperfect, erring man must pay for error by the letter of the law, the judge's cold adjudication, the mathematics of the fault, or by that other judgment of the fallible, imperfect, erring human heart.

That, sir, is the question for the jury . . .

And juries know the answer. Courts may state the law and counsel argue but the jury knows. The court rules that a contract, duly executed, shall be binding on the parties. The jury sees the contract, finds it duly executed. But there is something else . . . the jury sees: a hungry farm, a foundered plow horse struggling in a furrow, a man beside the struggling horse.

It hears . . .

turning, lifting his face to the jury

a man's voice . . .

Silence

cursing God

The jury tastes those raging words in its own mouth. It feels the sweating horse against its fingers. It is *there!*

pause

I trust my client's life to you — this jury. Not . . .

a bleak smile

to your pity! I cannot ask for pity and you have none. Not to your pity. To your indignation. To your rage.

You are the jury and you *know!*

You know what life is, the injustice of it.

You know the huge injustice of our death.

Scratch chuckles: Webster lifts his arm, levels it at Scratch.

You know what laughs at human suffering: it laughed at *you.*

You know the trap that closed on Jabez Stone: the same trap closed on you, each one of you.

You know it all: why Jabez Stone cursed God. You yourselves have cursed God, every one of you.

Silence — long silence

Gentlemen, I have one word still to say.

pause

Counsel for the plaintiff has suggested to you that something more than Jabez Stone is here on trial.

pause

That I am . . .

and my country which . . .

is also yours.

He thinks that if he tangles them all three together in a common case, so that a verdict for the one must be a verdict for the others, you will not find for Jabez Stone because you will not wish to find for me or for your country. He thinks, because you're dead and damned, you hate your country and all those who serve her.

Well, gentlemen, I challenge that assumption.

There may be much in our Republic which enrages you — I speak to you, sir, Colonel Burr. There may be much. But honest indignation is not hate. It scorns the false to find the true and so it learns to love the true. As you have learned, in death, to love your country.

Not, Colonel Burr, as you once thought, because she offered you an empire for your glory.

Not, as you thought, Captain Jim, because you made a fortune from her shame.

Not because God had given her to you — to *your* church and no other, Mr. Webb, as you believed on Boston Common.

Not, Mr. Lynch, because her lash kept order and you swung the lash.

Not, as every one of you once dreamed, because her new-found lands would make your fortunes.

Not even, as I told the Senate four months and nineteen days ago, because her destiny is greatness — because her trade will sweep the oceans and her power lead the world.

I was as wrong as any of you and more wrong. You learned the truth before me. Your indignation taught you in the night of Hell. Learning there to hate all human suffering you learned to love what

hopes, however faintly, for an end of suffering . . .

            a second morning of mankind.

pause

I trust your indignation, gentlemen.

I trust your rage to find for Jabez Stone — and
not in spite of the Republic but because of it.
You will not take the life of Jabez Stone to be
revenged upon your country. Rather, you will
save his life to show your country what she ought
to be — the one place on this sorry earth where
human misery will not be punished with more
misery — where even human folly can find hope.
You understand this, dead and damned, as no
smug jury of the righteous ever could.

He pauses, stoops a little, seems to look inward.

So much, then, for my country.

As for me, what counsel for the plaintiff tells you
is quite true, as is so much . . .

a wry bow to Scratch

                  alas . . .

                        of what . . .

he's said to you. I *am* on trial here. And not only
here but everywhere throughout New England.
And not on trial alone but tried — convicted —
sentenced. There is no need for you to find

against me: the world has found against me, my friends have found against me, even my hired man who is my wisest friend.

The best in Boston say I showed myself four months ago to have no care for human things, and least of all for human freedom, but only for the letter of the law, the letter of the Constitution. "Liberty," they say, "on Webster's lips is like the words of love upon a whore's."

reaching for a chair to steady himself

Gentlemen, I am an old man at my life's end and at the end dishonored. I know well what my place in history will be if Massachusetts writes the histories — and she will. I shall be called a traitor, not to my country only but mankind; a cold, unfeeling, devious politician who set the dogs upon the fugitives, the fleeing slaves — hunted them down along the northward rivers.

Well, we are damned together, gentlemen — and, no doubt, for cause. Thirteen damned men in a windy barn! We'd help each other if we could from common sympathy. Alas, there's nothing you can do for me: nothing but one thing — set the record straight . . . prove that on *this* night, before *this* jury, the man came first before the letter of the law. Prove that thirteen damned men, in this windy barn, fought for the freedom of a frightened, human creature as those who talk so loud of freedom never fight — snatched him from the jaws themselves of Hell!

Give me Jabez Stone to prove it and lift the hope of desperate humanity beyond the reach of Hell — the reach of Heaven — even beyond the reach of those who think themselves the surrogates of Heaven . . .

those priests of human freedom who would burn the country down to make men free . . .

ultimate hypocrites!

Silence, a long silence: he is near exhaustion.

Years ago, gentlemen, answering the first secessionists in Carolina, I gave the Senate a brief text by which to hope.

"Liberty," I said, "*and* Union."

I see now that I made it better than I knew:

Liberty cannot endure without the Union.

Union has no meaning without Liberty.

And Liberty is one by one — one man — each man — however weak, however desperate.

a long pause, head down

Give me Jabez Stone!

Defendant rests.

Scratch: Thank you, Mr. Webster. An eloquent address. Remarkable how many eloquent addresses are delivered when the cause is lost and evidence is lacking. Now, Your Honor, time presses, as you'll

see by that faint window. One never knows with
light like that when some ambitious cockerel will
choose to tell the universe he's up and so the sun
must follow. Once that happens, gentlemen like
those that grace this jury must be . . . elsewhere.

raising his voice

> *May it please the Court!* The parties rest. Per-
> haps the jury should withdraw to . . . *weigh* its
> verdict!

Hathorne: The jury will withdraw . . .

The jury disappears beneath the loft.

Scratch: Now, Mr. Stone, if you will take that chair. Make
yourself as comfortable as possible. Unfortun-
ately — not my doing, I assure you — not at all
— I'd have it otherwise and easier if I could —
unfortunately, the last human breath is like the
first — painful. At birth, I have been told, men
choke and scream in protest. I can understand
that. At the end they merely . . . choke.

He arranges Jabez's position in the chair.

> There! That's better, isn't it? We'll bring you
> through as easily as we can.

He draws his red bandanna over Jabez's face.

111

Now! Breathe as I direct you. Inhale. Exhale.
Deeply. Always deeply.

The jury, headed by Burr, returns.

Colonel Burr: *his gigantic pistol in his hand*

If Your Honor please, the jury has considered.

Hathorne: How finds the jury?

Colonel Burr: The jury finds for the . . .

Scratch: *In*-hale . . . *Ex*-hale . . .

Colonel Burr: . . . defendant.

Scratch: You have mis-spoken, sir. You said . . . defendant.

       a threatening step forward

Colonel Burr:

The jury gathering behind him, terrified but brave

The jury finds for the defendant and I so say.

Webster: *to the jury*

Thank you . . .

   long pause

Gentlemen!

The high, bright silver shriek of a cock. The chain of the door breaks. The huge door swings open. The room floods with sunlight. Judge and jury vanish into the cracks and crevices of the barn. Webster crosses slowly to Jabez, takes the contract from Jabez's hand, tears it to pieces.

Webster: Well, Neighbor Stone, looks like morning. With your permission, sir, I'll try the brook.

Perhaps a gaudy hackle underneath those alders . . .

You know I can't abide to be indoors when once there's light along the woodlots. I trust you will forgive an old man's crotchets.

to Scratch

And you, sir — shall we meet at breakfast? Breakfast at Cross Corners has no equal in New England . . . unless you'll grant me Marshfield. Jabez! I'll be back by seven. Three fried eggs and seven strips of that Cross Corners bacon to adorn my trout. Coffee.

He turns toward the sunlight from the open door.

Ah, the morning! The glory of the new-world morning! Untouched you'd say . . .

a grin at Scratch

since the Creation!

Scratch: *Untouched!* Examine it more closely, my exuberant friend. Bite the apple. Suck the plum. You'll learn a thing or two about your bright new world.

Webster: *back from the door*

Oh, I've learned a thing or two. I've learned that in America a man can face the Devil — even shake his hand — and still not lose his soul.

Scratch: Your soul! You've lost the *Presidency*, Mr. Webster.

Webster: I thought of that when you revealed the truth about my client and I decided to defend him, shame and all.

As I'll defend my country, shame and all . . .

my young Republic, westward of the world . . . with her dark flaw upon her!

Scratch: Of course! Your country right or wrong! We've seen your kind in Hell, sir: we'll see you.

Webster: Not my country right or wrong. My country with her wrong to right.

Scratch: By civil war!

Webster: No. By reason. And in peace.

Scratch: I trust you will forgive me, Mr. Webster. I suffer from a form of double vision which imposes sometimes on the present what is not present — yet.

It afflicts me now. I see a wounded army strag-
gling over red clay roads. I hear a voice shout. I
hear too what is shouted. "The Union forever!
Hurrah, boys, hurrah!" . . . And silence . . .
and no answer . . . and the guns.

Webster: Then you hear badly, Scratch, Old Scratch! I
hear the future shouting too. It says: "*Liberty
and Union*, one and inseparable, now and forever!" And the whole sky answers it.

*He moves to the place where we first saw him at the
beginning of the play.*

. . . now and forever . . .

Silence

Scratch: Liberty *and* Union! Chalk and cheese! Poor, de-
luded, cracked old man! What's Liberty? A day-
dream! Some frontier idiot in the frozen woods
watching the wild geese overhead and dreaming
he can follow them! *That's* Liberty — all the
Liberty there'll ever be. Union's the opposite —
the fenced-in barnyard; docile cattle, shoulder to
shoulder in the trampled mud.

That's real, the other's fantasy. Put the two together and you get . . . a fraud! Like your Republic!

Scratch, too, moves to the chair he sat in first.

115

You get civil war.

Jabez: *He has risen and stands where he was at the beginning of the play. He speaks to the audience.*

Mr. Webster believes in the Republic and that's enough for me. He believes that's what men are . . .

He is out of his depth and knows it.

bullocks in a herd and . . . well . . .

weakly

a dream of birds . . .

Scratch: You know, Jabez, I don't really care for you. It's only conscience keeps me laboring for your soul.

Jabez: *floundering and therefore bold*

A dream of birds.
He believes in it and *I* believe in it.

Scratch: You! You'd believe anything — even that you've seen the last of me.

Jabez: Maybe I have. It's morning. I'm still . . . here.

All three are motionless. Silence.